Poppy's Miracle

The remarkable story of a Greek rescue dog

Written by Michelle Foulia
Illustrated by Amanda Meaden

Poppy's Miracle
The remarkable story of a Greek rescue dog

Written by Michelle Foulia
Illustrated by Amanda Meaden
Cover & Interior Design by Michelle Catanach
Font: Dyslexie

First published in 2022
Copyright Michelle Foulia © 2022
All rights reserved.

ISBN: 978-1-7390991-0-7
Words for Healing

The rights of the author and illustrator have been asserted in accordance with Sections 77 and 78 of the Copyright Designs and Patents Act, 1988.

No part of this book or its illustrations may be reproduced (including photocopying or storing in any medium by electronic means and whether or not transiently or incidentally to some other use of this publication) without the written permission of the copyright holder except in accordance with the provisions of the Copyright, Design and Patents Act 1988. Permission has been granted from those who appear in the photographs at the back of the book.

Published with the support of TAUK Publishing.

To my children, for being a source of unconditional love and inspiration and for continually teaching me to be a better person.

To my husband, for never doubting my huge dreams and always cheering me on.

To every child...

You are enough, you will always be enough. Tune in to your superpower and soar.

Introduction

Letter to you, the reader.

Dear friend,

You hold in your hands a copy of my very first book. This book is about Poppy, our little Greek rescue dog.

I can't tell you how hard it has been for me to get this book out to you, something that should encourage you never to give up on your goals and dreams.

I was first inspired to write when I was around eleven years old, and I was leaving primary school in Cyprus, the country I grew up in. It was my last day of school and I remember my teacher, Mrs Nitsa, kneeling in front of me, saying that I had a gift — to write. She told me that I should keep a journal and write about my life and that one day I would write books that would help others.

I nodded politely, but I didn't believe her. I didn't keep my promise to keep a journal until many years later, when I was a mother and the need to write wouldn't go away.

Until the day Mrs Nitsa told me I had a gift, no one else in my life had told me anything positive about myself. I was used to being scolded for staring out of the classroom window and being lost in my imaginary world. I was always in trouble for being impatient, forgetful, easily distracted, unable to concentrate, and becoming angry because I couldn't adequately express my needs or frustration. I was also criticised and bullied for how I looked and because I had a lisp. The only person that saw something good in me was Mrs Nitsa. The words she spoke planted a seed in my heart, which grew over the following years, even when I didn't write.

Finally, when I passed my fortieth year, I began keeping a journal to help process my thoughts, unpack my feelings and order my mind. Then, in 2015, I was inspired to write this book because I wanted to raise money to help a friend create a therapy farm for children and adults who feel overwhelmed or struggle with anxiety, mental illness, disabilities, etc. as spending time with animals will make them feel better.

Writing Poppy's story not only helps raise money for the farm but also helps you, the reader, by showing you that miracles can happen. We must never give up hope or belief in our dreams and desires. Even when things seem to go wrong, there can be a lesson to help us grow stronger and wiser.

As a child, I didn't realise I had **ADHD**, Attention Deficit Hyperactivity Disorder. This essentially means that a person with **ADHD** cannot concentrate for long periods and usually has boundless energy. I see nothing wrong with that. I know I am capable of focusing. In fact, I can hyper-focus on things that engage me but struggle with conversations or matters that hold no interest. It's challenging when people require me to focus in school or work. It is a problem if there is mess at home and items get lost, or I forget appointments. But there are many positives that, in my view, outweigh the negatives and make me grateful to be just as I am; otherwise, I wouldn't have written this book.

Michelle Foulia

As I hadn't seen a specialist when I was younger, it was when my son Vangelis was assessed that I realised how alike we were and that **ADHD/ADD** was one of the reasons for my struggles. But beyond that, I also saw how **ADHD/ADD** has been a gift, as it enables me to be creative, write stories, think of ways to help others and be who I am.

I based the characters in this fictional story on our family and, of course, Poppy, who is sleeping by my feet as I type this letter to you.

You can learn more about Poppy and perhaps even meet her virtually or in person by visiting my website or following me on social media. There are many dogs like Poppy and so many families like ours, each with their own individualities and quirks. I hope our story will encourage, inspire and help you see that miracles are possible. You just need to believe and be patient.

I hope you enjoy the story and the journaling/drawing prompts that follow. Take your time and make this book your own in your very special personal way.

Stay inspired, believe in yourself and your dreams, become your best advocate, and know you are amazing.

Michelle

Chapter 1

"Alex!" shouted Mum. "For goodness' sake, choose **SOMETHING**. Otherwise, I will go straight ahead and pack whatever I like!"

"Why? Why do I need to choose anything? Why can't I just stay at home? I told you I don't want to go on this stupid holiday! Greece is hot and I don't like the heat, you know that. What's wrong with staying in England?" Alex threw the neat pile of clothes at his mum and stormed out of the bedroom.

An hour later, Alex sat in the car with his family, ready to set off. He felt bad. He didn't mean to shout at his mum, who had quietly packed his suitcase after his outburst. He had stormed off outside and ridden his scooter up and down the quiet street. This always helped him calm down when he felt angry. Why could no one understand him?

He glanced over at his mum in the front passenger seat, who was staring ahead, tight-lipped, quiet. He felt he had disappointed her... again. Just then, Dad's voice broke the silence.

"Right, we are ready to set off, folks. Are you all strapped in?"

Everyone started chatting enthusiastically, little Isabelle squealed with joy, and Mum fussed over her list to make sure nothing had been forgotten, but Alex's mind was elsewhere. He looked out of his window, his brow furrowed and his head resting on his hand.

He felt surrendered to his fate. There was nothing more he could do about it. He was going on this holiday whether he liked it or not. His big brother Nicholas and little sister Isabelle were annoyingly excited. They had gone on and on about this holiday for weeks, but all Alex could think of was leaving his comfortable room, which was laid out just as he liked it.

Since moving to a new house with his family a few months before, ten-year-old Alex worked hard to make his room just how he liked it. His sky-blue wallpaper has drawings of people skateboarding and doing parkour, his favourite activities, while the bunk bed, with the tent-like structure over it, felt like a den, his very own hideout. The bed had soft covers and sheets, and his weighted, comfortable blanket helped him feel calmer when things got too much. The switch meant he could control the intensity of the lights and make them dim whenever he wanted. Dad treated him to a TV and video game console for his birthday, and Nana Grace bought him a special gaming chair for when he played. He loved his room. It was his own little world where he could escape and relax. Everything had its place, even if it was messy. To Alex, it was just perfect.

Now he would have to deal with bright sunshine, which made his eyes hurt, itchy sand and scratchy bedding, and he couldn't have his video game console or comfy chair. Why did his family not understand how important those things were to him? He had heard his mum talking to his dad a couple of days before, after another storming-out moment. She said that she sometimes found it hard to deal with his **ADHD**.

ADHD. Four letters for four long words— Attention Deficit Hyperactivity Disorder. Alex hated these letters. He felt like someone had a huge sticker and plonked it straight on his forehead, like the only thing that defined him was his disorder. It seemed to explain how he struggled to sit still for long periods, concentrate on more than one thing at a time or pay attention to instructions. He also disliked the feeling of labels, certain fabrics, loud noises, bright lights, and even some foods that felt strange in his mouth. The word 'disorder' made him feel like there was something wrong with him, that he was different, that he wasn't 'normal' or 'in order'.

His thoughts jumped around his head while his eyes watched the passing cars full of different types of people, the tree-lined streets, the ugly grey bridges, and the seemingly endless motorway.

Finally, the car came to a stop at traffic lights. Alex glanced out of the window and across the road to a park on the other side. In the distance, he could see a group of school children shouting and jumping about excitedly. He squinted his eyes to get a better look. It didn't take long for him to see why there was so much apparent excitement.

A fight had broken out, and the children were encouraging the two opponents against each other. A lump formed in Alex's throat, and tears stung his eyes. He knew how that felt. His eyes scanned the park and pavement. People were going about their business like nothing was happening. No one wanted to get involved. His shoulders slumped, and his gaze dropped, saddened by the whole situation.

Suddenly a faint smile appeared on his face. If there was anything good about this stupid holiday, it was that he was going to be away from Jason, the school bully, for two weeks. Two weeks of not getting up in the morning with knots in his tummy. Two weeks of not giving up his lunch money to Jason and going hungry. Two weeks of not having to carry the shame of being unable to tell anyone.

He settled back in his seat. *Maybe this holiday isn't such a bad idea, after all*, he thought as he popped on his headphones and pressed play on his phone. Little did Alex know what lay ahead for him and the whole family.

Chapter 2

"Stop pushing me, Alex," whined Isabelle as Alex almost threw her through the entrance to their holiday apartment. He thought they would never get there with all the queuing, waiting, walking, more waiting, screaming children, loud announcements and a boring flight. He had been stuck in his seat for hours.

"Alex, be patient, please," Mum reproached.

Alex tutted in frustration, desperately trying to restrain himself from catapulting his little sister from the front door and through the open patio doors that led to their apartment balcony smack bang in front of the beach.

"Well, get inside then!" was all Alex could utter before his older brother Nicholas pushed both of them in and barged past to look at the view. Alex's face started to turn red, and he clenched his fist and bit his lip in his best attempt not to shout, punch or kick at his brother. He knew it could blow his chances of getting on that beach.

"Oh, my goodness, would you look at this view!" Nana Grace exclaimed, and everyone stopped and stared ahead.

There in front of them, beyond the open door and marble-floored sitting room, the patio doors framed the most amazing clear, cloudless, blue sky, joined by a turquoise sea. It was almost impossible to see where the sky ended and the sea began as the blues blended harmoniously. While everyone stared in silence for a few seconds, children's laughter could be heard from the beach below.

Alex's senses came alive all at once, processing the various smells, sounds, and feelings. ADHD can make a person feel more intensely, and Alex was trying to see, hear and feel everything all at the same time. The irresistible saltiness of the sea entered his nostrils as he took in a big breath.

"Can we go to the beach now, Mum, please?" he shouted.

"No, Alex, I'm afraid you can't, not just yet. It has been a long day of travelling, and we need to unpack our luggage, work out who is sleeping where, put our things away, find a place for dinner, have a ...."

"But Mum!" Alex interrupted impatiently. "By the time we do all that, it will be night-time. Can I go by myself? I'll be fine."

"Yeah, right, you'll be fine," Nicholas jumped in. "You know how you always find a way to get yourself into trouble. Knowing you, you'll end up falling, drowning or drowning someone else."

"You can be quiet. No one asked you!"
Alex yelled.

Mum dropped the bags and glared at Alex and Nicholas, her jaw clenched with both hands on her hips. Just as she was about to speak, a loud thud came from one of the bedrooms. Everyone ran to see what it was.

Dad was unpacking the swimwear and had been trying on his new goggles. The label hanging, still intact, was covering one of his eyes. While rummaging through the suitcase, he popped Isabelle's now inflated, pink armbands on his wrists to allow him to carry on searching for the rest of the family's swimwear. In his effort to reach the dressing table to put the sun cream down, he tripped over the suitcase strap and fell with a loud thud. By the time the family ran in to see what happened, Dad was sitting on the floor, goggles still on, pink armbands around his wrists, looking like a superhero gone terribly wrong.

Everyone burst into laughter just as Nana Grace came running in from her bedroom wearing a bright yellow swimsuit covered in lots of white plastic daisies that had been sewn on. Her large straw hat was hand-decorated with even more matching daisies. This, of course, made the family laugh even more, although Nana Grace was not amused.

Mum sighed. "I suppose if Dad is happy to take you kids down to the beach for a play and some exploring, Nana and I can unpack the cases and get everything in order here. We'll meet you downstairs in two hours. Then we can go look for some food."

"Yay!" Isabelle cheered and quickly set about collecting all her beach toys. Alex and Nicholas shoved each other as they tried to walk through the apartment entrance at the same time. Dad glanced over at them, and they knew not to push the boundaries any further.

Down at the beach, they were met with a plethora of sounds, smells and sights. The sun was so bright and warm it made Alex's eyes water and his skin tingle. He shut his eyes to help adjust to the brightness and sounds of people's laughter, splashing water, birds chirping, music from the beach bar and busy chatter from sunbathers. He took a deep breath to smell the saltiness from the sea that he had experienced just a few minutes before in the apartment. It was such an unusual smell, and he could taste it too.

A big smile formed on his lips, and he stood there for a few seconds wanting to feel everything. He felt happy now that they were finally here. Jason, the bully, seemed millions of miles away, and Alex decided to put him out of his mind for the duration of his holiday and enjoy the opportunity to be free from the bullying and teasing. Jason had noticed how Alex would suck the tops of his tee-shirts and would tease him. *'Forgot your dummy, have you?'* How could Jason understand that sucking the fabric brought him comfort? It felt nice in his mouth and gave him something to occupy his unbridled energy. But he wasn't going to ponder on that now. He was going to make the most of this holiday.

"Hey, kids, come on. Let's go explore this place." Dad's voice echoed from further down the beach.

"Coming, Dad," replied Alex as he ran to catch up with him. The word 'explore' filled his imagination with all sorts of possible adventures, not for one moment realising the adventure that lay ahead a few hours from now.

Chapter 3

"Wow, this is delicious! What is it?" exclaimed Mum, with her mouth full.

"Bou - ga - tsa," replied Nana Grace, proud of herself at being able to pronounce it. "It is a Greek pastry filled with custard and cinnamon. It was left in our welcome basket with homemade jam and some fresh lemonade. Here, have some."

Mum took the glass of lemonade and sat on the sofa, her shoulders drooped, with a sad expression on her face. Nana Grace put her arm around her.

"Look, I know it can be hard to deal with Alex's impatience and persistence and stubbornness and all that, but honey, you need to ease up a bit. He is doing his best, you know. It's not easy going through all these changes, especially with his **ADHD**."

Mum's shoulders relaxed as she sat back more and stared at her feet.

"I know, Mum, I know. But sometimes, I just can't find the energy or strength. I love him so much, I love everything about him, his kindness, his sensitive heart, his fiery spirit, but I find it hard to love his **ADHD**."

"Ah, but sweetie, all those things you just mentioned *are* part of his **ADHD**. In fact, they are all part of who Alex is!" Mum looked up at Nana Grace as if she had said something profound.

"I have never thought of it like that."

"Yes," Nana continued, "we may put labels on behaviours we do not understand, but that's what we do to help us understand better. Alex's ADHD, as we call it, is what makes him so smart, sharp, creative, kind, generous and passionate. We need to remind ourselves of this and celebrate his differences and uniqueness, not criticise them. I'm sure he already gets a lot of criticism in school. Here at home, we need to do our best to embrace it and help him learn the tools to manage the challenging aspects. We all have challenges; we just don't have labels for them. It's us who need to change our hearts, our understanding, our tolerance and patience and work with Alex to help him deal with his challenges. I wish I had done that with you and your siblings instead of getting frustrated or worried that you would not succeed. You remind me so much of Alex when you were his age."

Mum was thoughtful, and she looked back down at her feet. Nana stayed quiet and held Mum's hand in her hands. A tear rolled down one of Mum's cheeks. Then another.

"You are right. I know you are. I need to search within my own heart to find and practise the understanding and strength to be a better mum."

"You are a great mum," responded Nana Grace. "None of us can be perfect. There is no such thing. We are developing our character and the attributes that help us become more content with where we are. We need to love those around us as they are and not try to change them." Mum nodded as she wiped her tears with her hands. Nana Grace took Mum's hand. "Honey, all you have to do is remember to try and see the world the way he sees it so we can come alongside and support him and help him grow into the amazing person he is becoming. We need to celebrate him and his amazing gifts." Mum looked up, thoughtfully at first, then with a grin.

"Right, come on then, Nana. Let's go and find them and get some food. I'm starving!"

Everyone met as agreed down at the beach outside the hotel. Isabelle had been collecting seashells and proudly showed them to Mum and Nana Grace. The boys were covered in sand from a sand fight, which was no surprise, but Mum chose not to comment or reproach them. They started to walk along the beach to find a restaurant for dinner. Little did they know, they were in for a big surprise!

Chapter 4

"What is going on over there?" called out Nana Grace with a concerned look on her face. Everyone turned to look. "Sounds like dogs fighting, but I hear a man yelling too. Do you think he is being attacked by dogs? Let's go help him, quick."

Dad rushed ahead, and by the time the family caught up, he was talking loudly to an elderly man, and looking rather silly, flapping his arms here, there and everywhere in an effort to communicate. The elderly man was surrounded by dogs of all sizes and shapes. Some were yelping, others were eating greedily out of huge plastic bowls, and some bossy ones were chasing off the weaker, smaller dogs so they would get more to eat. Alex held his hands to his ears to block some of the noise.

"What's going on, Dad?" Nicholas asked, staring at the elderly man.

"Meet Mr Takis, guys. He is the restaurant owner and feeds the stray dogs in the area.

That's what the commotion was about. I say we eat our dinner here and show our support to him for being so kind and feeding the stray dogs." Dad was clearly decided about eating here, and as everyone was so hungry, they did not argue.

During dinner, the family chatted excitedly, trying different traditional specialities, guessing what they contained, while Alex played safe and ate chips and a little salad. From where he was sitting, he could see the spot just further away, where Mr Takis fed the dogs. He watched as a small, furry, grey puppy attempted time and time again to get some food while the bigger dogs snapped at it until it cowered away. However, hunger would not allow the puppy to give up, so it would try again and again, each time managing a morsel or two but retreating into a corner when told off by the other dogs. Alex dropped his fork and thought. He was reminded of how Jason, the school bully, treated him just like the big dogs were bullying the puppy because it was small. Alex was small too and often wished he was bigger like his brother Nicholas.

Alex took a sausage from one of the main plates in the middle of the table. He held it under the table and made a gentle clicking noise with his tongue, hoping to catch the puppy's attention. The bigger dogs were so busy snarling at each other that they did not hear him, but the puppy did. It turned its head around and immediately spotted the tasty sausage in his hand. Slowly and nervously, it approached him, weaving through tables and chairs and other diners. Once under the table, it gently reached over and grabbed the sausage. As soon as it was securely in its mouth, it seemed to disappear down the puppy's throat in two seconds flat! The puppy then reached over and licked Alex's fingers. Just as Alex was about to reach for another sausage, Mr Takis spotted the puppy under the table, shooed it away, and the puppy scarpered. Mr Takis apologised to the family and explained that if he allowed stray dogs to come to the dining area, he would lose customers as it was unhygienic. Not everyone liked animals or wanted to be pestered, but Alex was cross and worried. He hoped the puppy would be OK.

"Mr Takis, what are the chances of the dogs finding homes?" he asked.

"Ah, almost impossible, my little friend," Mr Takis replied. Alex chose to ignore the term 'little' and continued.

"So, what happens to them? Where do they sleep? Are they safe?"

"Well, my father owned this restaurant and always fed the strays. He would say that he was blessed to have the opportunity to own his restaurant and provide for his family, so the least he could do was to help someone else, in this case, the stray dogs. Now I run the restaurant and continue to feed them. They are often abandoned here by people who bought them as cute puppies and then thought that they were hard work, so dumped them here on the beach. But they can always find food, and as long as I have good health to run my restaurant, these dogs will always have something to eat."

"Wow, that is so gracious of you," piped up Nana Grace. "We are honoured to eat at your restaurant, Mr Takis. Well done."

As the conversation continued, Alex slipped away. He followed the puppy to see where it would go. It had slid under a bush by the side of the restaurant and curled up in a little bundle in an old cardboard box with a bunch of rags inside. As Alex tried to sneak up, he tripped over a small rock in the ground and fell, almost landing on the cardboard box. The thud frightened the puppy, who ran away yelping, while Alex's family came running to help him. They found him blushing and making various excuses, but he had hurt his knee. Mum decided it was time for the family to retreat to their apartment and get some rest.

Alex, however, couldn't get the puppy out of his mind. Would it come back to the cardboard box? Would it be safe tonight? Would the other dogs bully and bite it? Would there ever be someone to give it a loving and safe home? It wasn't fair that dogs became homeless in this way because of irresponsible owners.

Chapter 5

The brightness of the Greek sunshine woke everyone up early. Alex squinted while trying to open his eyes. In the kitchen, Nana

Grace was making toast and smothering it with the homemade strawberry jam from the welcome basket. She smiled at Alex and offered him some toast. Alex thanked his nana, examined the jam carefully and then tucked in, noting how tasty it was but not making any comment. Instead, he gazed through the open window at the ocean, his thoughts competing for space in his head.

"Alex?"

"Err, yes?" Alex noticed Nana looking at him with one eyebrow raised. Oops, she was onto him.

"I know that look, Alex. You are up to something. What are you working on, my sweet mischief?"

"I am thinking about the puppy, Nana," Alex blurted out, almost relieved to get it off his chest. "You know the puppy we saw last night at the restaurant? She is so lovely, Nana, and Mr Takis said that it was unlikely she would ever find a home. Those other dogs were bigger and older than her and, from what I saw last night, not very kind towards her. She is small and in danger." Alex was now more animated, his face almost touching Nana's for full effect as he delivered his last sentence. "Someone needs to give her a home. I think it should be us!"

"Oh, darling boy, you have such a sweet, compassionate heart, but our family doesn't have the money to take a dog to England. There are all sorts of things it needs. A vet to examine her, vaccinations, a permit to go to England, flights, all that costs a fortune! Besides, if you really want a dog, isn't it better to get one from a shelter in England? There are many beautiful dogs in the shelters, all needing a loving home.

That's if you can get past your mum, of course."

Alex's shoulders dropped, and he put the rest of the toast back on the plate, pushing the plate away from him.

"Yes, getting it past Mum...," he murmured and walked out of the kitchen.

The rest of the day was spent on the beach. Mum chased everyone with the sun cream, while Dad was inflating various swimming armbands and rings. Nana read her book under the shade of an umbrella, Nicholas sunbathed while listening to music with his earphones on, and Isabelle collected seashells and screamed for help every time sand blew in her face.

Alex allowed Mum to cover him in sun cream without the usual objections and spent most of the time floating on his inflatable bed, arms gently paddling the warm sea water. He allowed his mind to wander, imagining life back in England with the puppy and all the fun they would have. Maybe he could even teach her skateboarding; he'd seen a dog on TV doing that!

At the end of that busy day, they decided to return to Mr Takis's restaurant for a meal. Alex was excited at the thought of seeing the puppy again. He had the fastest shower ever and was ready before everyone else—a very unusual occurrence. Usually, the whole family had to wait for him. Mum noticed but did not say anything. She also noticed how quiet and thoughtful Alex had been all day at the beach, even letting her put sun cream on him, which he usually hated. When they were all finally ready, Alex shot out of the apartment and into the lift, holding it open for everyone else.

"Well, what a gentleman you've suddenly turned into, little brother!" scoffed Nicholas. "What are you after?"

"Nothing, I can be kind if I want to," replied Alex, resisting the urge to be rude to Nicholas for calling him 'little' and starting an argument. He knew he could jeopardise their visit to the restaurant or end up getting him grounded at the apartment for the evening. Nicholas made a hand gesture which meant he was watching him, but Alex looked away. He was trying hard to control himself when everything in him wanted to punch Nicholas.

While walking to the restaurant, Alex did something he hadn't done before. He looked up at the sky and made a wish. He didn't know if it was a wish or a prayer, but with all the sincerity in his heart, he desired that he would find the puppy and that somehow, he could make it his own.

"Alex, are you alright?" His mum's voice startled him.

"Yeah, sure I am, Mum. Why?"

"Well, you are awfully quiet today. Has something happened?"

"No, well, yes, well, not exactly happened, I was just wondering…."

"Well, hello to my new favourite family of customers!" Mr Takis interrupted. Alex's shoulders slumped. How was he going to approach this question with his parents? How was he going to convince them to adopt this puppy?

Over dinner, Alex was restless. The puppy was nowhere to be seen. Where was it?

What if something terrible happened? Just then, Mr Takis approached their table.

"Are we ready for dessert? My wife makes the most delicious baklava on the island."

"Ba- kla - what?" Isabelle asked cautiously. She was not one to ever refuse dessert, but this sounded very strange.

"Oh, you do not know? It is the most famous dessert in Greece, no? Layers of crispy pastry with crushed pistachio nuts, cinnamon and honey. Mmmm." Mr Takis pretended to lick his fingers one by one, which made everyone giggle. Shyly, Alex finally asked the question.

"Mr Takis, where is the puppy tonight?"

Mum looked over and immediately knew why Alex had been quiet all day. He had been thinking about the puppy! How could she not have realised? Alex had been asking for a dog for years and they had promised to consider it once they were settled in their new home, but then life got busy, and they never discussed it. With Mum being so tidy and constantly worried about germs, she avoided the subject of a dog even though deep down she knew it would be good for Alex to have a pet. When they met the puppy yesterday, it was obvious Alex was completely besotted with her.

"Ah, the puppy," answered Mr Takis. His eyes looked down at his feet while his eyebrows came together, almost meeting in the middle. "She is not well. When I came to open the restaurant this morning, I found her injured on the step there. It looks like one of the bigger dogs has bitten her. There is a big wound. I cleaned and bandaged it, but I don't know if she can survive. She needs to be in a home with people who can take care of her. I can't do that; I am at the restaurant too many hours with my wife and children."

"Oh no!" Nana Grace looked worried. "Where is she?"

"I placed her in a bigger box with a blanket on the other side of the restaurant where the other dogs don't go, but I can't guarantee her safety."

Alex couldn't control himself any longer and blurted out. "We'll look after her, Mr Takis, won't we, Mum, Dad? We'll take her to our apartment and keep her safe until her leg heals!" Before Mum or Dad could answer, Mr Takis jumped in.

"That is fantastic news, my little friend! Absolutely wonderful! How can I thank you? I know. Some free baklava and ice cream too from your friend Mr Takis."

Mum glared at Alex while Dad sat there with his mouth open, unable to think of what to say. Alex looked at his mum pleadingly. Tears formed, and he tried to hold them back. Mum's heart immediately softened.

"I guess it wouldn't be a huge problem to take care of her for a few days while she recovers. But if she misbehaves, yelps, or disturbs the neighbouring apartments, or I find any toilet business on the floor, she is coming back here, Alex. Do you understand? We have to be responsible and honourable to the people renting us the apartment."

Alex could hardly believe it. "Yeah, Mum, I understand. Don't worry. You won't hear a peep out of her, I promise."

When they all finished their meal, they followed Mr Takis to the large box at the other side of the restaurant where the puppy was resting. She looked sorry for herself, not even budging when the strangers approached. Her head was buried in her tummy as she was curled into a ball with her foot bandaged up. She had managed to chew through the dressing and lick her wound, which made it worse, and the bandage was haphazardly hanging off. Alex lowered himself gently and placed his hand in front of her nose. She sniffed it nervously and then lifted her head, suddenly looking perkier. She recognised Alex from the night before when he offered her those juicy sausages. She licked his hand, and he stroked her head.

"Looks like you made a friend there, little girl," Mr Takis commented.

"Why does he have to call everyone little all the time? Alex thought in frustration. *Little girl, my little friend. Argh!*

Alex lifted the puppy gently out of her box and wouldn't let anyone help him. Dad carried the box, and the family slowly walked back to their apartment, where they made the puppy comfortable for the night. Alex insisted on sleeping with her to ensure she didn't cry at night or go to the toilet on the floor. Mum knew this was very important to Alex, so she allowed him to sleep on the sofa next to the box with the puppy in it.

Gradually, one by one, everyone drifted off to sleep, but Mum was worried. Staring at the ceiling, she whispered, "What do I do now? He is going to get attached to this dog. How are we going to be able to hand her back and go back to England? Why do things have to get so complicated?"

She got out of bed and went to check on Alex. She found him fast asleep on the sofa with the puppy curled up next to him, her head resting on his arm. Mum stood there for a few minutes with a smile on her face. *Ah well, I know it will work out...somehow.* With that, she went to bed, wondering what she would find when she got up the next morning. Would the puppy even be okay?

Chapter 6

Mum's eyes opened at the bright sunlight coming in through the curtains. She shot up out of bed, aware that the apartment was quiet, and they'd seemingly had an uneventful night. Rushing to the living room, she found Alex with Dad on the balcony cleaning the puppy's wound and laughing at how she kept pulling at the bandage to play. Nana Grace had just made fresh coffee. Isabelle was eating breakfast while watching Greek cartoons on the television, and Nicholas was still asleep. As soon as the puppy saw Mum, she wagged her tail.

"Ah, don't you try to get into my good books, you cute little thing." Mum playfully tickled her belly while Dad and Alex looked at each other but stayed quiet. "I know what you two are thinking," Mum said. "No, I am not going to grow attached to her. She is only here for a few days."

As Mum walked back towards the kitchen counter to pick up her coffee, Dad glanced at Alex and gave him a wink. Alex smiled and continued wrapping the fresh bandage.

"I think we should take her to the vet today," Dad said. "Just to make sure there is no infection. She also needs a name. We can't just call her 'the puppy'!"

Everyone seemed to agree, and a short taxi trip later, in the vet's waiting room, a lively discussion ensued with all kinds of names being suggested. Favourite television characters, famous Greek foods, even Greek human names, except the family didn't know many and could hardly pronounce the ones they had heard.

"What about something easy to pronounce, but something that also reminds us of Greece? What have we seen that we can connect to Greece?" said Mum finally.

Quiet filled the room. You could almost hear their brain cogs turning. Nana Grace looked around until her eyes stopped at a large picture on the wall. Her frown turned into a huge smile. She considered for a moment or two, and by the time she spoke, the others had followed her gaze to the picture. It was a framed drawing of wild poppy flowers. The drawing was in grey pencil, the same colour as the puppy, even though poppies are usually bright red.

"Poppy!" they all said at once.

Isabelle shouted out, "I love it, I really like it! Yeah, let's call her Poppy! Hello, Poppy!" The puppy wagged its tail, approving her new name. There were clearly no objections, so it was decided Poppy would be her name. At that precise moment, the vet called them in. Little did they know, but they were in for another surprise.

In the examining room, the vet smiled and patted Poppy, who was sitting still and being as sweet as honey. The vet asked lots of questions in very broken English, and the family just nodded politely, unable to understand a single word. What they did understand was that the vet went back and forth to her fridge filled with medicines, gave Poppy some injections, popped a pill down her throat, put some drops on her neck, cleaned the wound on her leg and produced a booklet with the words *'Pet Passport'* on it. By the time they realised what had happened, Poppy had been fully vaccinated, wormed, treated for fleas and had her very own passport ready to fly! Politely, the vet handed the bill to Dad, patted Poppy and waved them all goodbye.

"What just happened?" asked Dad when everyone was back in the taxi.

"I am not sure," was all Mum could utter.

"I think the vet thought we adopted Poppy and are taking her back to England. She must have been asking us if we wanted her vaccinated and prepared for flying," responded Nana Grace.

After a few moments of silence, the whole family erupted in fits of laughter. Alex became very solemn.

"Why don't we take her back with us? I mean, we've done all this now, right? Can't we just take her?"

"Son, as much as I would love to say to you, *"Yes, let's take her*," it isn't that simple. There are rules for flying dogs to other countries and it costs a lot of money. We agreed to look after her until she is better, and we have ten days left on our holiday here so by then she will be fine, I am sure. Who knows, maybe she will find a family to adopt her now that she has a name and all her vaccinations in place." Dad spoke with finality, indicating there was no point in discussing any further. But Alex still had hope.

"So, are you saying that if it wasn't for the cost, you would let us take her home to England?"

Dad looked like he had just been caught stealing some sweets. "Err...well, emm...I...hmmm." He cleared his throat and looked at Mum, his eyes pleading for her to get him out of the situation he had just got himself into. Mum picked up the hint.

"Maybe. I don't know. Can we just get home, please, and try to make the most of what is left of our day? I want to check out the local market."

Chapter 7

When Mum arrived at the local market, she was overwhelmed with the hustle and bustle. Shoppers were negotiating prices for their goods in loud voices and with their arms flailing everywhere. The deafening honking of horns from motorbikes and cars trying to squeeze through the impossibly narrow lanes made Mum step as far back from the pavement as she could.

At the market, she marvelled at the bright purple stacks of shiny aubergines, dark green courgettes, sherbet orange from the piles of oranges and clementines, and all the food smells mixed in with fumes of cigarette smoke. She decided to have a coffee at one of the local cafés in the market and chose a seat right at the back where it was quieter but could still observe the energy of the hurly-burly at this busy market.

As she sipped her coffee, she thought back over the years she had raised her children and the different challenges, the frustrations in dealing with Alex's ADHD, the doctors, consultants, specialists and even mental health counsellors they visited. Each had their own advice and their own list of exercises, techniques and medication. She then thought of Nana Grace's words. Were she and Alex's dad trying to change Alex? Were they missing out on his gifts and beautiful personality among the busyness of trying to 'fix' him'? The conviction hit her hard, and tears started to roll down from her eyes.

She loved Alex with all her heart but suddenly became aware that she was inclined to tell him off more often than she was ready to encourage, reward or praise him. She had fallen into bad habits too, and now, on this holiday, her son had fallen in love with this little dog. His compassion overruled any logic about how Poppy could even go home with them or the cost of the journey. His heart wanted to save this dog, and that's all there was to it.

Instead of seeing his compassion and need for a furry friend, she had been stern and strict and determined not to let the dog soften her own heart. After all, she had been telling the family for years that if they ever got a dog, it had to tick all her boxes. It couldn't moult, yelp, jump up and down on people. They couldn't choose a puppy because she didn't want mess in the house or stuff to be chewed and destroyed. It had to be a rescue dog from a shelter, already vaccinated and neutered and assessed for suitability with children.

Mum shuddered, realising how unwavering she had been at her impossible list and at the grace shown to her by the family who knew there would never be a dog that fitted all those requirements.

Now, here they were, with a little rescue stray puppy, all the opposites of her list, yet this little dog had made its way into Alex's heart and was slowly making its way into the hearts of the whole family. But, even if she relented and wanted to take the puppy back to England, how on earth were they going to find the money to do it? And with so many shelters back in England full of beautiful, wonderful dogs needing homes, were they even justified in taking a dog from this country back to theirs?

With all that in her mind, she was determined to let things take their course. If this puppy were meant to go back to England, she wouldn't stand in the way, but somehow, she knew it would take a miracle.

Later, back at the apartment, Mum called a family meeting. Everyone was nervous as it usually meant someone was in trouble or a new decision needed to be made. Alex was more nervous than everyone else. The last time they held a family meeting was when Mum and Dad announced that they were moving to a new house, meaning Alex had to leave his friends, his neighbourhood and all that he held dear. Was this going to be about Poppy? Was it Mum's way of telling him that Poppy had to be returned to Mr Takis now she was better and with just a few days left of their holiday? His eyes filled with tears as he braced himself to face the family. But he was about to be astonished.

During the meeting, Mum explained she had been a bit harsh in giving out a huge list of prerequisites that a potential dog should fulfil in order to be adopted into their family and that maybe the dog for them had made its way into their lives without them even realising. At that, every mouth in the room was left open. They could hardly believe what Mum was saying.

"Mum, are you actually saying that we can keep Poppy?" Alex asked, his eyes huge like saucers.

"Well, not exactly, well, sort of...." Mum hesitated. "The problem, Alex, is that it's near impossible to get her to England. You see, there are rules and laws we must abide by to get her there, and this costs money. But what I'm saying is that I'm willing to make enquiries to see if it is even a possibility. But please don't get your hopes up. It's a long shot, and it wouldn't harm trying to get the word out there for any possible homes for her locally."

Alex didn't even hear the last sentences. He decided that Poppy was going back with them, and he would do everything in his power to get her home. He jumped out of his seat and launched at his mum, giving her the biggest, tightest hug in what seemed like years!

"Thank you, Mummy," Alex whispered as he nestled his head in her chest.

Surprised, Mum kissed him on the head as tears rolled down her cheeks. It had been a very long time since he called her 'Mummy', and it felt good.

The following day, Mum set to work. Dad was still not convinced. They had achieved this holiday on a tight budget, and there was just no extra money to get Poppy to England, no matter how much the family had grown to love her. But Mum was determined, and she visited the local internet café and searched online for companies that transported dogs to

England. Several calls later, disheartened, she headed back to the apartment to report the bad news.

"The cost is too high, guys. We would need to drive Poppy to Athens, which is six hours from here. This means hiring a car, and they are not cheap. We need a special crate for her that will cost at least 130 euros and then we need to get her on the flight to England and return here for our own flight from the local airport. But what's worse is this: the flight is 1,000 euros! We just don't have that kind of money. Not to mention that we would have to arrive home and drive to London to pick her up, which is five hours from our house, and I am not sure our old car would cope!"

Alex's heart sank.

"Well, there has to be another way then," Nana Grace piped up. "What about animal welfare charities? Our neighbour adopted a dog from Spain not that long ago. How did they get the dog over to England?"

"Good point, Nana," Mum said. "I'll go back to the internet café and do some more research. I'll meet you all at the beach as soon as I can."

A couple of hours later, Mum came up the path that led to the sunbeds where Dad, Nana Grace and the children were relaxing. They left Poppy resting in the apartment so as not to get sand in her wound; it was now healing up nicely. She was such a good dog. She never barked or cried when left and would ask to be taken out for her toilet needs—remarkable for a puppy, especially a stray.

"OK," Mum reported. "I found a dog shelter near Thessaloniki about an hour and a half's drive from here. The lady who runs it is lovely. Her name is Amanda, and she has created this amazing shelter in the mountain. She wants to help us if we can't get Poppy home and is happy to look after her until we save more money or find a solution."

"This is great news," said Nana Grace.

"It is good news, but we need to look at solutions to get Poppy home as soon as possible. Amanda told me about a charity based in England with an office in Greece. They rehome stray dogs from Greece in the UK. They want to help us!"

"How can they help?" asked Dad.

"I told them about our predicament, and they said they use a company that transports their dogs by road, not aeroplane. They have a vet onboard to make sure the dogs are kept safe and well during their trip. The dogs are fed and walked and taken care of. It takes three days to bring the dog to England, but it costs a quarter of the price! What's even better, they will take Poppy to England for us and let us pay them back little by little, as and when we can."

Mum continued. "There are further problems, though. They don't have room for her on the next trip out, which is in three days, and they don't have another trip for another month. Amanda will keep her for us until the next trip, but she needs to be taken to Amanda's shelter, and I'm not sure we can make that. Plus, we would need to collect Poppy from London when she arrives, which is a long way from our home and would cost a lot in petrol, aside from the uncertainty that our old car would make it."

There was silence as they all made their way to the apartment. Everyone felt defeated. Alex slumped in his seat, and Poppy placed her head on his lap, licking his hand. She had grown to love her new family, but she knew something was wrong. *Was she going to be thrown away again like last time? Was she not good enough for her new family?* She rested her head, closed her eyes and wished for everything to work out. Alex stroked her, his tears disappearing into her soft grey fur. His silent tears became sobs, and when Mum finally made her way to him, he threw his arms around her and cried inconsolably. It all seemed to go so well. Now it was all going terribly wrong. The holiday was coming to an end, and soon he would return to school and Jason the bully, without his beloved Poppy. How could this be happening?

Suddenly he felt an arm around him. He turned to see Isabelle handing him her favourite stuffed rabbit toy, the one she had loved and held since she was born six years before. It had never left her side, its ears lovingly stroked and worn by Isabelle's little hands.

"Here, Alex," she said quietly. "You can have Rabbit. She'll keep you company wherever you go, and she'll love you always. She is the best friend you could ever have."

His little sister's gesture deeply moved Alex. He had never really paid much attention to her, and she seemed to be more an irritation than anything else, but he was astounded by her incredible act of kindness and generosity. He knew how important and precious her rabbit was to her. He also realised that Isabelle understood how much Poppy had come to mean to him and how she wanted to soothe and comfort him. A warm feeling engulfed his heart, and a smile formed on his face.

"Thank you, Isabelle, that means a lot to me, but I think Rabbit is happiest with you." He handed Rabbit back to Isabelle and pulled gently on one of her bunches in a friendly way.

There were just two days remaining of the holiday, so the family decided to visit Mr Takis for dinner and update him about Poppy. Mr Takis was also sad as he had hoped that, at least for this little dog, there would be a new life, a new future. But he had not given up.

"We must continue to believe, my friends," he said cheerfully. "Miracles happen all the time all around us, and you just never know when you might get your very own miracle." He concluded with a wink of an eye while serving a round of Greek strawberry ice cream. Strangely, this brought a smile to everyone's face, and they left for the apartment in better spirits, feeling more positive and somehow hopeful.

The next morning, Mum sipped her coffee on the balcony while everyone still slept. Poppy sat at her feet, gazing out into the ocean. Suddenly, the mobile phone rang. It was the charity.

"Hello, Mrs Jones, we have some good news! Our van, which is leaving tomorrow for England, has had a cancellation and we have one space free. We would like to offer it to Poppy!"

"What?" Mum gasped. "That's amazing! Oh, but just a minute, the thing is, we can't get her to Thessaloniki in time."

"Oh, no worries, I've sorted that! I never realised, but the driver has to pass your town to get to Thessaloniki, so we can pick her up from you," the lady replied enthusiastically.

"Wow, that is truly wonderful! I can't thank you enough. *We* can't thank you enough." But then, suddenly, Mum paused. "I'm really sorry, but I know we have one more problem, and you have been so kind to us. I am not sure how to tell you this."

"What's the matter? Tell us. If we can, we will help. We have got this far to get Poppy home. I'm sure we can help if there is a way."

"Well...my husband says we can't pick her up from London. It's too far for us to get to and we don't have the petrol money to travel all the way there and back when we get home. It's a five-hour drive each way, and our car is old and can't go far. I'm so sorry, I just wish... you know we never intended to get a dog like this, and now...." Mum was lost for words, and she felt so terrible. The lady on the other end assured her that she would make enquiries to see if they could help any further and get back to her as soon as possible.

"It may be possible for a volunteer to drive Poppy from London or even meet halfway. I'll make some enquiries. Let's not give up yet."

Mum hung up the phone but chose to say nothing to the family as she did not want to get their hopes up.

Soon, they were all up, dressed and had breakfast, ready to hit the beach. Mum asked Alex if they could take Poppy for a walk together instead of joining the others on the beach. Alex was delighted to join his mum, and he didn't feel like doing anything else anyway and wanted to spend every possible moment with Poppy. Secretly, Mum was hoping that the phone would ring with good news, but she felt she needed to prepare Alex for the possibility that they would have to leave Poppy behind with Mr Takis.

They started their walk along the seafront under the row of palm trees. Mum was trying to find a way to start the conversation, looking for the right words, when the phone rang. It was the lady from the charity. Alex sensed his mum's unease and became nervous. What if it was bad news? What if Poppy couldn't come home with them? Was this the end? He glanced up at his mum and tugged her sleeve, but she signalled with her finger for him to be quiet, which only served to irritate Alex and make him more anxious.

"Mum, what is she saying?" Alex pressed. Mum ignored him and continued listening to the voice at the other end.

As Alex was about to snatch the phone from her hand and scream at the woman on the other end, Mum hung up and turned to face him, a solemn look causing him to hold his breath.

"Well, Alex, we gave it our best. We put up a good fight, and we sure didn't give up." Alex's eyes welled up, anticipating the bad news he was now expecting. "And it was all worth it!" Mum squealed, jumping up and down. "Poppy is coming home. Our family has now officially grown by one. Poppy can leave tomorrow, and the charity will bring her near to our home as their final destination. The vet on board the van lives fifteen minutes from our house. What are the chances of that happening?" Alex stood numb, trying to take it all in. Mum continued. "And once we are back, they will send one of their volunteers to come and visit us to make sure Poppy is settled in, and we are informed of all that she needs to be happy and well cared for."

Mum was now crying, the relief evident on her face. She grabbed Alex and squeezed him so tight he too burst into tears, almost unable to believe that finally, everything had fallen into place. Poppy was coming home, and everything they went through had worked out in the end.

Poppy watched the scene and began jumping on Mum and then Alex, rejoicing at their joy as if she understood she now had her forever family and would never know hunger or fear again. They ran back to find everyone on the beach, and when Alex told them the great news, they cheered with amazement. Naturally, they made their way to the taverna and shared the news with Mr Takis, who did not look surprised.

"I told you, my friends," he said, "miracles can happen, even for a little dog. We just have to believe in them."

And then he winked.

Journal / Draw / Reflect

The following pages are space for you to use as you wish. I created it to allow you to let your mind wander, your thoughts pour out, and let your creativity unfold on these pages in the way you feel most comfortable.

You may wish to use the prompts, write your own, or just write, draw, doodle, or free flow with no prompts.

There is no right or wrong way to do anything here. You can just leave it blank. You may choose to return to it at a later time or never. This book is yours to use as you wish. No one needs to see it, so make it your own in whatever way feels good to you.

Michelle Foulia

I stopped worrying about how to write Poppy's story and instead let my hand do the work, my mind flow and my heart connect to the pen (or keyboard, ha-ha).

Poppy's Miracle

What did you think of the story?

Michelle Foulia

Poppy's Miracle

How did the story make you feel?

Michelle Foulia

Poppy's Miracle

Who was your favourite character in the story and why?

Michelle Foulia

If you could rewrite the story, what would you do differently?

Michelle Foulia

Whether or not you have been diagnosed with **ADHD** or know someone with **ADHD**, I hope this story helped you understand it is not something bad but simply a word that certain people choose to identify a set of traits and behaviours.

Everyone is wired in unique ways, and some are given names like **ADHD**. Even though many do not understand it, that does not make it bad. In fact, as an adult and a mother with **ADHD**, I now realise that it is a gift. There are so many things I can do that my friends can't.

I am very creative, inventive, imaginative, kind, compassionate, positive and sensitive to the needs of others.

Remember how Alex didn't like the word 'disorder'? I don't like it either. But if I can't change the words others use, I can change how I think about the special qualities that make me, me.

Think about **ADHD** as a beautifully wrapped box filled with many gifts. Open it up and look inside. All these gifts make **YOU!** They help you think the way you do and be the amazing and wonderful person you are.

There are some ideas below. You can circle them, colour them, or even add your own.

Poppy's Miracle

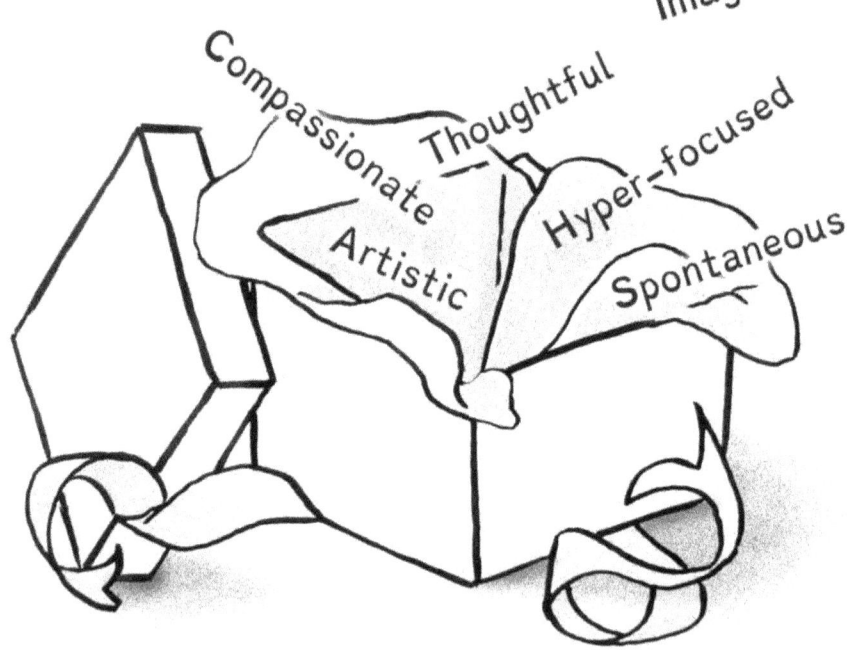

Michelle Foulia

What name would you give to the qualities that make you the person you are?

Some would describe certain emotions, thoughts and behaviours as negative because they can generally cause difficulty. For example, trouble with concentration can make it difficult in school when we need to focus on the lesson.

Other difficulties may be: being easily bored and needing to do something else when others are happy watching television or sitting in a restaurant, watching a sports game, concert, theatre play, or even at the cinema. These are not bad or negative behaviours/emotions. You simply need to move more often than others.

So how can you manage those emotions?

Here are some ideas. Add your own or circle/colour the ones you resonate with.

When I feel angry, frustrated, bored, impatient, need to move my body, can't concentrate, (insert your own) _____

I can...

Stretch my body even from a seated position—thinking of one muscle or limb at a time, tightening it up really tight and then releasing it and feeling it relax.

I can start with:

- 🐾 curling my toes tightly and releasing

- 🐾 curling my feet tight and releasing

- 🐾 stretching my legs out tight and releasing

- 🐾 squeezing the muscles in my tummy and releasing

- 🐾 arching my back forward and then backward and releasing

- 🐾 closing my fingers into a tight fist and releasing

- 🐾 pulling my tight fists in at the wrists and releasing

- 🐾 hugging my body with my arms as tight as possible and releasing

- 🐾 holding my hands together and stretching my arms out in front of me, above my head or as far back as I can get them, feeling the stretch in my body and releasing

- 🐾 moving my neck around in one direction gently and then the other and releasing

- 🐾 scrunching up my face while closing my eyes as tight as possible and releasing.

This is called progressive muscle relaxation, and you can do it any time you feel the need to move or relax.

Take deep, slow breaths, counting to whatever number I can reach while breathing in, holding my breath as long as I can, then slowly counting in my head as I release the breath. Focusing on counting my breaths helps my mind relax, become calm and refocus. I will do that until I feel a sense of calm return.

Doodle on a notepad or blank page, whatever comes to me. Often doodling helps me listen better as my hands are busy, and therefore I can concentrate better.

Write out my thoughts and worries as they come so that I know they are safely captured on paper and, therefore, out of my mind so I can focus better.

Use my imagination to travel to any place I want to: build my favourite house, go on holiday, invent something, participate in a favourite activity. If I am not in class and let my mind wander freely, I can take time to address every detail of the places and things I imagine. Such as:

Colours	Smells	Air
Forms	Feelings	Sunshine
Design	Touch	Rain
Shapes	Heat	
Tastes	Cold	

Even in the most boring places, I can travel anywhere and be anything without anyone knowing. This is how the most successful artists, inventors and writers create their stories, inventions or paintings.

Communicate to those around me when I feel I need to take a short walk. If I'm in class, this can be to the bathroom and back, or if I am in a restaurant or aeroplane, I can stand up, stretch and walk up and down a little.

Communication is very important because it lets others know how you are feeling and what you need at that moment. Communicating your needs before you become frustrated ensures you do so calmly and thoughtfully as long as it is not deliberately distracting to others.

Picture a bunch of balloons and give each a colour of your choice. In each one, place your thoughts, frustrations, annoyances, and emotions, then imagine you are blowing them away and watch them in your mind as they float high up into the sky, taking your worries, frustrations and anger with them. You might prefer to picture them as little explosions, a boat taking all those thoughts as cargo, a hot air balloon, a space rocket, a torpedo, a submarine, whatever you wish.

What have you found helpful in the past?

Write it down and keep it like a box of tools ready to use anytime you need to.

Poppy's Miracle

In the story, Alex wouldn't give up on getting Poppy home. In the real story (at the end of this book), my son Vangelis refused to believe that Poppy may not return home to England with us. He absolutely believed with all his heart that she would somehow make it back.

Although sometimes, our plans don't work out, it does not mean we stop believing in our dreams. It does not mean that we give up. Our mind is a very powerful organ, believing whatever we tell it. Many of the world's most successful athletes, actors, TV personalities, scientists, authors and others achieved their dreams through sheer belief even when it seemed impossible.

Even when others around you tell you your dreams are impossible, don't stop believing in them. Somehow your mind will lead the way to fulfilling those dreams and ambitions, but you must remain faithful, trusting and believing. It does not mean that we can wish for anything and simply have it. The laws of nature and order are at work, but it means that you have not been the obstacle in your quest. Ultimately, when we have believed and done all the right things to achieve something, and it doesn't work out, we must trust that our path is different and that a benevolent force at work is simply guiding us to it.

Write your dream here. Describe it or draw it in as much detail as possible. What does it look, smell, feel and taste like?

Experience it in your mind and heart as you describe or draw it and picture yourself there. Feel the moment. Who is with you? Are there people cheering you on? Is it night or day? Are you holding an award? What are you wearing? What is the weather like? Truly place yourself in that dream, close your eyes and savour it for a few moments. You may wish to tear this page out and stick it on your bedroom door or mirror so that you are reminded of it daily.

Remember: believe and trust in the outcome.

Poppy's Miracle

Michelle Foulia

When you feel ready, go back and reread the story. Using your pen, pencil, coloured pencils, crayons, or whatever you prefer to write/draw with, circle or underline words and sentences that make an impression and make you feel something as you read them.

You might feel a tightness in your tummy. Circle, underline or maybe write in the margin what you think made your tummy react in this way. Was it the word or the description? Did you identify with it? Did it feel familiar? Did it make you sad or happy? Did it remind you of something that happened to you?

Journal about it in the margins or the space here or draw a picture. Journaling or drawing helps you unpack your emotions. Imagine a large suitcase filled tightly with so many clothes you can't tell what is underneath the top layer. As you take each item of clothing out (this can be each emotion, thought, feeling, or memory) and put it aside, you can see what more is underneath. As you remove each item, you are making space, and before you know it, the suitcase is empty, and you can easily find everything you are looking for.

Ask those thoughts or feelings why they are there. If you feel sad, ask yourself, why am I feeling sad? Do I know how Alex felt being bullied? Feeling sad isn't bad, and there is no good or bad feeling. Feelings are there to help us recognise what is going on so we can love and care for ourselves more and help others because we know how they feel.

If you feel anger, then ask yourself why. You may want to write or draw about your anger or choose a trusted person in your family, school, or friends to share and, again, unpack what is making you angry.

Recognising our emotions, feelings, and thoughts helps us process and understand them and ourselves better. Butterflies in our tummy, our heart skipping a beat, our face feeling flushed, and our palms getting sweaty are all ways our bodies react to our emotions or thoughts. They can be signs of fear, sadness, excitement or anger. Only you will know by investigating your feelings.

I mark all of my books. I write in margins, circle and underline words because it helps me understand what I am reading and how it makes me feel. Use this space to write or draw whatever you want to.

Michelle Foulia

Poppy's Miracle

What do I do with those emotions?

Once you have identified how the story resonated with you and the emotions you unpacked, you may want to explore further. You can ask for help from a trusted family member, teacher, school counsellor, or friend.

Often, simply identifying and understanding what you feel, where in your body you feel it and what causes you to feel that way helps you connect better to yourself and know yourself even more, like a best friend. In turn, this means you can take care and protect yourself, act before you feel rage, and nurture your mind and body.

I have written some ideas of what you can do with different emotions, but you may not like mine, so feel free to come up with your own.

When I feel **sad,** I can search my heart to find out why. Maybe I need to apologise for making someone upset. Perhaps I need to forgive someone. Maybe, I am missing someone who is no longer here with me. I can write them a letter even if they never see it. I can write and pour out all of the stuff inside me that makes me sad. I can draw a picture and pin it on my wall or throw it away once I am done. I can make a gesture of kindness for someone else. I can listen to my favourite music, watch a favourite movie, cuddle my pet, go for a walk, or meet a friend who makes me laugh. If I can't change what is making me sad now, one day, I will be able to, and that's OK. In the meantime, I shall be kind to myself.

Michelle Foulia

Write your own preferred methods.
When I am sad, I can...

When I feel **angry**, I can count as high as I can until I feel my anger calm. I can exercise by: going out for a walk, running, riding my bike, or if I can't go out, I can do jumping jacks in my room, jogging on the spot or doing press-ups. Exercise helps release the anger and extra energy and helps my body and mind calm. I can draw different emojis or words on pieces of paper and stick them on my door to let my family know that I need some time alone, a hug, or uninterrupted time with a family member. I can visit: a grandparent, aunt, uncle or friend to talk. I can write a letter to my parent expressing how I feel if talking is difficult. I can write a letter, pour all my anger out, and then destroy the letter. I can draw an angry picture.

Michelle Foulia

Write your own preferred methods.
When I am angry, I can...

I have written a list of emotions on this page for you to consider. Use this page to show how you feel about something or read each word and see how you feel. Again, as before, write next to it, above, below, or anywhere you like.

You may want to make a list and cut out the words on the paper. You can then stick them on your bedroom door, so others know how you are feeling, even if you can't tell them.

Michelle Foulia

For the last journal prompt, take your time and write a letter to yourself.

Write whatever you like. Perhaps how the story of Poppy's rescue and Alex has helped you understand yourself better or how you felt when you didn't know what would happen to Poppy. You can write what you have learned and how the story and journaling prompts have helped you.

Michelle Foulia

If you want to write me a letter, I would be delighted to know what you thought of the story and how it helped you, what you would have done differently...anything at all. I value your opinion.

I thank you for reading this book, and I want to honour you for the person you are. Remember, we were never born to fit in but made to stand out! You have unique qualities to bring to this world, so own who you are, embrace your journey, be willing and humble to learn from your experiences and grow in wisdom and valour. These are the gifts you will serve the world with. Don't try to be like anyone else. Just be the best you can be because there is only one of you in the whole wide universe. Isn't that incredible? So why would you want to change that?

I send you love, light, grace and peace.

Michelle

Do you want to know Poppy's real story?

Read below.

In 2015, our little family of five lived in Katerini, Greece, for one year. During that time, we fostered two sisters, so our family became seven. It was a demanding but wonderful time. However, it was about to become even more challenging when I received a call one day from a friend.

"Michelle, I go swimming every day on a deserted beach for exercise, and there are many stray dogs being fed by a restaurant owner. Today I noticed a puppy maybe 3-4 months old among the older and bigger stray dogs, and I think she would be perfect for you."

"Thanks, Harry, but I am not looking for a dog."

"Well, I think she would be perfect for the kids. She seems really sweet."

"Yeah, but I don't think I can cope with a dog right now, and besides, if we were to get a dog, I would get it from a shelter where it had already been vaccinated, neutered, wormed, and assessed for suitability with children. Also, there is **NO WAY** I am getting a puppy. I have enough to cope with. I don't want a dog peeing everywhere, barking and jumping up and down on us and licking our faces."

"She is soooo sweet, Michelle. I worry that the older and bigger dogs will kill her when they compete for food. They were snapping at her when I was there."

"Oh Harry, really, we can't take on a dog. Tell you what, though, I'll go and look at her and see if I can think of anyone who may want her."

That was my 'fatal mistake'. It was pouring rain, and as soon as I arrived, without any prompting, this little puppy spotted me and ran over to me. To my astonishment, she didn't jump on me but sat by my feet, looking at me as if pleading to be stroked. I bent down and picked her up, expecting to have my face licked, but she didn't. She looked at me, gave me one solitary lick on the hand, and I instantly fell in love.

I knew right there and then that she was meant to be ours. Just a year earlier, while still in the UK, I had a vision of a dog just like her. Now, I knew I was being prepared for her arrival into our lives.

After a conversation with the restaurant owner, I left her and returned the following day with my husband and all the children to surprise them. After parking the car, I walked over, picked her up, and brought her to the children, who were screaming with excitement. We drove straight to the vet in town, had her vaccinated, wormed, checked all over, purchased supplies from the vet's shop, and went home as a family of eight.

Her name was decided in the car. I suggested we choose a name that was easy to pronounce for our Greek-speaking foster children and everyone else—a name that would remind us of the countries that have been home, Greece and England. The children shouted suggestions, and suddenly as we drove past a field with wild poppies, everyone shouted, "Poppy!" and so it was.

Poppy had her first bath and settled in on the first night. There was no crying, chewing, or peeing! During the night, she went to the toilet in the bathroom right next to the toilet. How did she know? There was no jumping or licking our faces or yelping. She was, and is, the sweetest dog we could have ever wished for and is perfect for a family of children with different needs and challenges.

Poppy settled into our lives as if she belonged there all along. There was no adjustment, no difficulties, and no transition. It was the most remarkable experience to witness. Everyone who met her fell in love with her. Friends whose children had dog phobias brought them to overcome their phobias, and her sweet-natured gentleness always won them over.

She is a remarkable little dog.

Then, catastrophe!

Three months later, our circumstances changed dramatically, and we needed to return to the UK. Finances were dire, and we just about scraped the money together for airfares and a deposit for an empty rental property we hadn't even seen.

Our foster children went on to another home, and as a mother, I was busy organising, packing, preparing, and comforting the children, helping them with their sudden changes and transitions, and trying to hold it together myself and be strong for everyone.

But what about Poppy?

We looked at flying her to the UK but finding the money for the cost was unachievable. We just did not have that kind of money, not even for the crate or to drive her to Athens as was required.

Our son Vangelis, who was seven, stated that if Poppy couldn't come to the UK, he would stay in Greece, sleep with her in the garden and look after her. For him, with his various physical and psychological challenges, she had been like a therapy dog, and he was deeply attached to her.

My husband was not negotiating. He said she needed to be rehomed and that we had a lot to deal with. I was stuck in the middle. I sent out a prayer and asked for help.

The following two weeks, before our departure, marked a series of events that had to be seen to be believed. Truly unbelievable. With each possible solution came an impossible obstacle, and we would think she wasn't coming home. But something would happen to give us hope, a glimpse of a light, only for another obstacle to appear. And on and on, it continued right up to the last moment. Just three days before our flight home, a miracle happened, and Poppy could come home with us.

We arrived back in the UK to an empty, cold shell of a house on a winter's day — a Friday, in December 2015, days before Christmas. Friends rallied together to bring us second-hand furniture, beds, kitchen utensils, and food. By Sunday, the house began to look more like a home, and we drove to Liverpool, just twenty minutes from our house, to collect Poppy, who had been travelling by van for three days through Europe with a vet escort on board.

With Poppy safe, we returned to our home and a new chapter began.

A few weeks later, we visited a very close friend, Marie, who had bought a property in North Wales. She wanted to create a therapy farm where anyone who needed to visit and be with animals and nature could go with no charge or criteria.

As she described her vision of wanting to use her vast experience of working as an occupational therapist to provide a safe, restful, loving place that would bring comfort, solace, and joy to those struggling with life, I knew I had to find a way to help make her vision a reality.

That is when the idea came to write a children's book about Poppy's story.

The book would give hope to children everywhere that miracles can happen. Even for a little dog, hope never dies. We must never give up on our dreams and we must be open to whatever life brings, even if it doesn't fit our criteria.

At the same time, I wanted the book to raise money for my friend's vision. I wanted to help make it a reality and fund other projects that rescue, rehabilitate and rehome dogs. I also wanted to contribute to charities like the one that helped us get Poppy home against all odds.

The photos below are the first photos I took of Poppy. The first three were taken the day I went to see her on my own, and the rest are when we took the children to meet her.

Michelle Foulia

Poppy's Miracle

Michelle Foulia

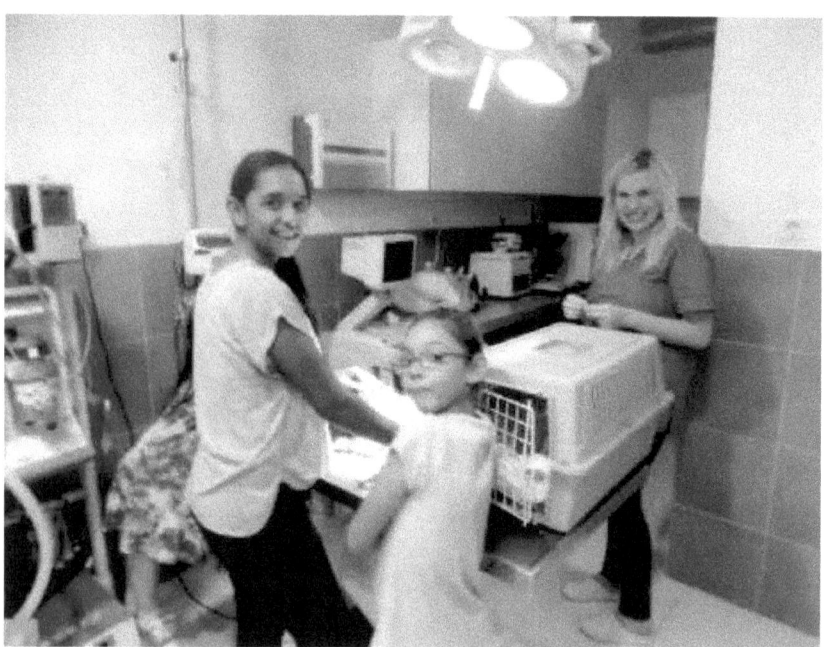

Poppy Today

As I type these last words, Poppy is fast asleep on the sofa. It is November 2021, and Poppy is six years old. She is a delightful little dog, truly a gem in our family. We could never have wished for a more lovable, sweet-natured, gentle dog. I know she was meant for our family. We have grown in wisdom and love because of Poppy, the experience of her rescue and adoption into our family.

Poppy now shares the sofa, bed and all other parts of the home with Melon, the cat. They are both very happy and regularly welcome friends to our home with wagging tails and requests for treats.

The only time we remember that Poppy was once abandoned on a beach in Greece is when we travel by car, and she refuses to sit on the car floor. She becomes panic-stricken and will only settle on our lap or the car seat. We don't know what she experienced back then, but now she has a family that has loved her ever since and will love her to the end of her days.

Many stray dogs and cats are roaming the streets in countries like Greece. There are stray dogs living in shelters in every country in the world, including the country you live in. You may not see them in the streets, but the shelters are full. Perhaps, if this story inspires you, you will consider adopting a stray dog from a shelter. If that is not possible, you can sponsor a dog by contributing to its food and veterinary bills until a family is found. You can also donate food, blankets and toys to a local shelter or call them and ask them what they need. You may even be able to volunteer with a parent to walk or cuddle shelter dogs. If you are going on holiday, research the animal welfare charities and relevant numbers before you go so that if you find a stray animal, you can get the help it needs.

You can keep in touch with me and Poppy through my website.

www.wordsforhealing.org

Poppy's Miracle

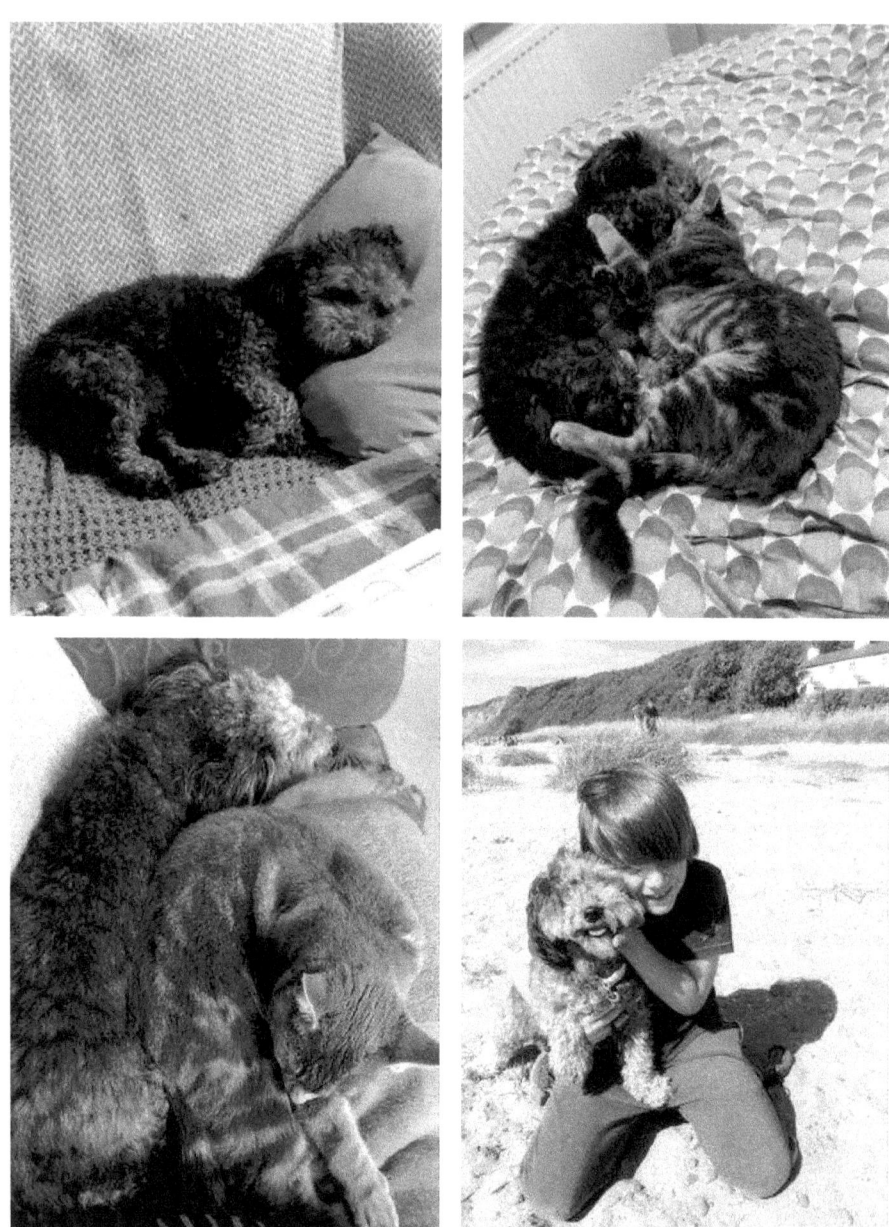

Acknowledgements

It will be impossible to thank everyone who has helped me in some way or other in the completion of this book, and fear of leaving someone out has led me to decide to omit names. What is important to note here, however, is that there have been many people over the last few decades who have encouraged me to write. There have been strangers who were inspired by our conversation, family telling me I inherited the writing gift from my deceased parents and paternal grandfather, and friends who have read my blog posts, Facebook posts, emails, letters, and poems and insisted I had to write books.

My primary school teacher planted the seed. Chance encounters, synchronicities and coincidences watered it. But the ground was already prepared and the desire to write never left me. What I lacked was a belief in my abilities and the potential for my books.

Over time, each voice continued watering the seed until it sprouted and grew. It has taken 37 years, but here I am, and not without each and every one of those voices who never gave up on me.

Thank you.

Thank you for injecting your belief into mine, for financial help to make this book possible, and for your messages, cards, and calls.

Most of all, of course, I am grateful to my husband and children, who have witnessed the struggle, the doubts, fears, procrastination, and for never for one second doubting my ability to realise my dream of writing books that heal the world.

Michelle Foulia

My wish and prayer are that I can inspire them and you, the reader, to push past those negative mind-voices and pursue your dream, whatever it is. It was planted within you for a purpose and is gestating through your experiences, but only you can birth it.

I must extend deep-felt gratitude to Amanda from Compassion for Greek Paws, whose encouragement and positivity upheld me while trying to find ways to get Poppy back to England from Greece. She dedicated her life to rescuing and rehoming dogs in Greece, and her memory lives on through the work of her family, volunteers and, in a small part, this book.

Greek Animal Rescue made the impossible possible and helped us get Poppy home. As I type this, they have just three volunteers covering the entire country of Greece. While they are inundated with calls for rescues, they juggle full-time jobs, parenting and life.

These incredible humans who give up their time and energy selflessly to the rescue of animals deserve not only recognition and gratitude but practical and financial support. It is my hope that this little book will help in some way towards their invaluable work.

Marie Crawford, who has been a long-time friend, confidant, and mother figure in my life, has also kept watering that seed for me to write. She has picked me up more times than I can count with her encouragement, belief, love, and kindness. Some years ago, she sold everything to purchase a smallholding in North Wales. She had the vision to create a small therapy farm and, using her experience as an occupational therapist, provide a safe, loving place for children and adults to connect with the animals and beautiful nature and experience their healing power. Hafod Moor Alpacas (www.facebook.com/HafodMoorAlpacas) inspired me to write Poppy's story so that I could raise funds to make her vision come true. I hope it does.

My heart is full. I am happy, grateful, satisfied and ready for the next chapter.

About the Author

Michelle Foulia was born and raised in Cyprus. After the death of her parents at age five, animals became her closest companions leading her to volunteer in animal welfare and her studies in animal-assisted therapy, counselling and psychotherapy.

Her struggles in foster care, the loss of her guardians, and battle with **CPTSD, ADHD** and Fibromyalgia have cultivated a deeper compassion, understanding, and desire to make a difference in the lives of others. Writing has been her therapy, which naturally birthed the vision to write books that make a difference. Her company, Words for Healing, is her vision to write and publish books that heal the world one book at a time. She also coaches people to write their stories and encourages them to create an impactful message.

Michelle now lives in Wales with her husband, three children, her cat and, of course, her dog, Poppy.

www.wordsforhealing.org

www.ingramcontent.com/pod-product-compliance
Lightning Source LLC
Chambersburg PA
CBHW040241130526
44590CB00049B/4114